# Lady Jane Grey

*by Simonetta Carr*

with Illustrations by Matt Abraxas

REFORMATION HERITAGE BOOKS

Grand Rapids, Michigan

**Reformation Heritage Books**
2965 Leonard St. NE
Grand Rapids, MI 49525
616-977-0889 / Fax: 616-285-3246
e-mail: orders@heritagebooks.org
website: www.heritagebooks.org

Library of Congress Cataloging-in-Publication Data

Carr, Simonetta.
  Lady Jane Grey / by Simonetta Carr ; with illustrations by Matt Abraxas.
      p. cm. — (Christian biographies for young readers)
  ISBN 978-1-60178-190-1 (hardcover : alk. paper)  1.  Grey, Jane, Lady, 1537-1554—Juvenile literature. 2.  Great Britain—Kings and rulers—Succession—History—16th century—Juvenile literature. 3.  Queens—Great Britain—Biography—Juvenile literature.  I. Abraxas, Matt, ill. II. Title.
  DA345.1.D9C37 2012
  942.05'3092—dc23
  [B]
                                        2012023845

For additional Reformed literature, request a free book list from Reformation Heritage Books at the above address.

*Printed in the United States of America*
17 18 19 20 21 22/10 9 8 7 6 5 4 3

# CHRISTIAN BIOGRAPHIES FOR YOUNG READERS

This series introduces children to important people in the Christian tradition. Parents and schoolteachers alike will welcome the excellent educational value it provides for students, while the quality of the publication and the artwork make each volume a keepsake for generations to come. Furthermore, the books in the series go beyond the simple story of someone's life by teaching young readers the historical and theological relevance of each character.

## AVAILABLE VOLUMES OF THE SERIES
John Calvin
Augustine of Hippo
John Owen
Athanasius
Lady Jane Grey
Anselm of Canterbury
John Knox
Jonathan Edwards
Marie Durand
Martin Luther
Peter Martyr Vermigli

# Table of Contents

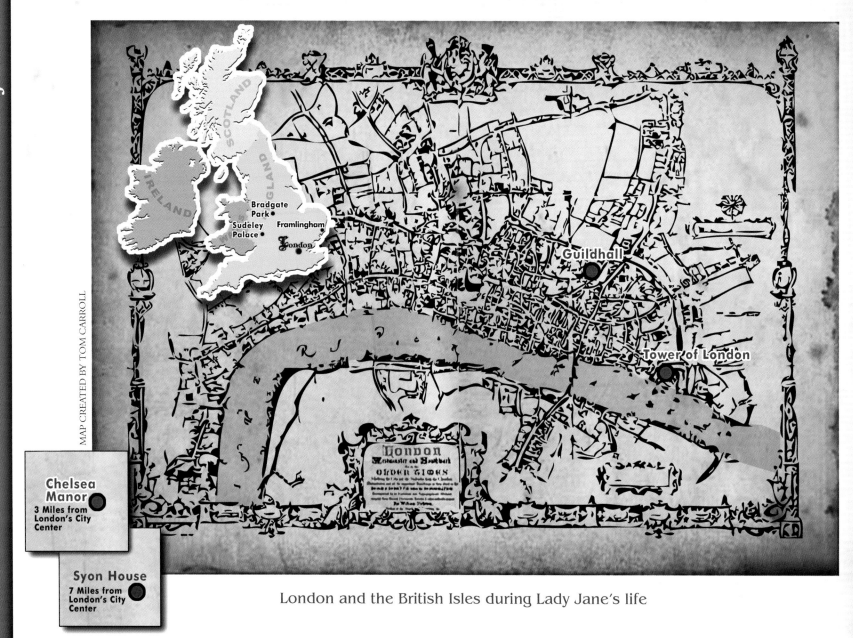

MAP CREATED BY TOM CARROLL

SCOTLAND

IRELAND

ENGLAND

Bradgate Park •

Sudeley Palace •

• Framlingham

London

Guildhall

Tower of London

**Chelsea Manor**
3 Miles from London's City Center

**Syon House**
7 Miles from London's City Center

London and the British Isles during Lady Jane's life

# Introduction

Lady Jane Grey lived almost seventeen years and ruled England for less than two weeks. Still, she has been remembered for generations for her courage in defending the gospel until the end.

To understand Jane's life, we have to remember that she lived at a time of great changes. Until a few years before her birth, most Christians in Europe obeyed the teachings of the Roman Catholic Church, which was led by a man called a pope. Over time, many popes had become distracted with riches and power and had paid less attention to the teachings of the Bible.

Many Christians were unhappy with this situation and tried to bring people back to the simple message of the gospel, which is the story of what God has done through Christ for sinners. Today we call these people Reformers.

No one knows exactly what Lady Jane looked like. There are many portraits, but there is no proof that any of them show the real Jane. This drawing was inspired by one of these portraits.

King Henry VIII

England had been under the pope too, but just a few years before Jane's birth, this suddenly changed. Henry VIII was king of England at that time, and his wife was Catherine of Aragon. The king wanted the pope to end his marriage with Catherine. When the pope refused, Henry decided he didn't need the pope's approval. Instead, he declared himself head of all English churches and expected all his subjects to believe and worship as he did.

King Henry changed the English church radically. For example, he closed all the large buildings where monks, friars, abbots, or nuns lived together and tried to put a stop to many teachings about life after death that were not based on the Bible.

The Ruins of Whalley Abbey, one of the religious buildings closed by Henry VIII

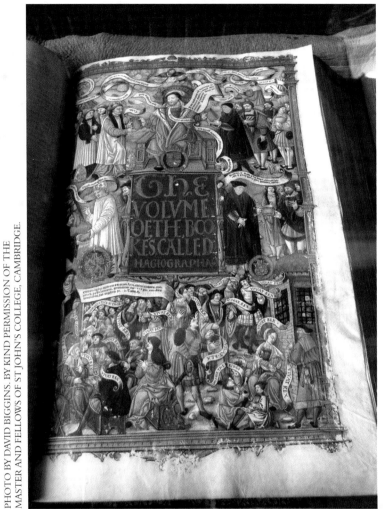

A full page from a section of King Henry's Great Bible, the first authorized Bible in English. This section was actually about the history of great men and women of God. It shows King Henry VIII on his throne, presenting two Bibles—one to the leaders of the church and another to the people.

Henry also allowed the distribution and use of English Bibles, which had been forbidden for many years. Until then, the Roman Catholic Church in England had insisted that the only Bibles available should be in Latin, not in English. Since only a few educated people read Latin, few people could read the Bible. The church services were also in Latin, but Henry started to introduce some in English.

On the other hand, King Henry didn't agree with all the teachings of the Reformers, and some were still considered illegal under his rule. In fact, people could be arrested and sometimes sentenced to die for some of these teachings. When someone is killed as a punishment for something illegal, we say that he or she is executed. Probably Jane, as a young girl, heard about people executed for their faith, because some were famous.

Henry VIII still considered some of the Reformers' teachings illegal, and those who spread them were arrested and sometimes sentenced to die. As a young girl, Jane probably heard about some of the famous people who died for their faith, like Anne Askew, who was executed when Jane was about nine years old.

CHAPTER ONE

# Raised to Be Queen

We don't know the exact date or place of Jane's birth. We know that she was born sometime in 1537 and spent most of her life in a large country home in a forest area called Bradgate Park. Her mother, Frances, was

KEVIN TALBOT

Bradgate Park

the king's niece, and her father, Harry, was a rich nobleman who was interested in the latest studies and discoveries. He liked helping students and preachers, so Jane's house was always full of fascinating people. Harry and Frances were only about twenty years old when Jane was born. Later, they had two more daughters.

The ruins of Bradgate House, where Jane used to live

A few months after Jane's birth, the kingdom celebrated a very exciting event! King Henry and Jane Seymour, who was his wife at that time, had a baby boy, and they named him Edward. It was a time of great joy because the king had long waited for a son to take his place on the throne! Sadly, Jane Seymour died only two weeks after her son was born. In those days, people didn't know as much as we do today about cleanliness and infections, and women often died soon after they had babies.

As Lady Jane Grey grew up, she probably visited the royal palace from time to time, where she met her important cousin. Both children were smart and studied under the best teachers. In fact, Edward's teachers were so good that King Henry didn't seem to mind if they believed and taught the gospel as it was explained by the Reformers.

Lady Jane received a similar education. Since the Greys were closely related to the royal family, her parents taught her to behave like a princess. As most parents at that time, they were strict with her.

Prince Edward and Young Jane

In January 1547, when King Henry died, his son, Edward, became king under the name of Edward VI. He was only nine years old. Before dying, King Henry had appointed a council of sixteen men to help his son rule until he turned eighteen. They, in turn, appointed one of the young king's uncles, Edward Seymour, to act in his place. The most important and influential men on this council agreed with the teachings of the Reformers and thought that it was the right time to introduce them to England.

King Edward VI

COURTESY OF HERITAGE HISTORY (WWW.HERITAGE-HISTORY.COM)

The excitement spread to other Christians all over Europe. At that time, people had to follow their ruler's religion, so many came to England from other countries to worship according to their faith.

Thomas Seymour

In the meantime, just one month after King Henry's death, Jane was invited to live at the house of Edward Seymour's brother Thomas. In those days, many noble families sent their children to stay with other noblemen, where they could get an excellent education. Thomas was now married to Katherine Parr, who had been King Henry's last wife.

Katherine and Thomas had fallen in love some years before, but because King Henry asked her to be his wife, and refusing a king would have been very unwise and dangerous, they had not been able to marry. Now they were free to be together again. Their home was always busy. Not counting the visitors, over 150 people usually lived with them.

Jane liked Katherine, who was a very kind woman with a special love for children. Jane and Katherine shared a passion for books, fine clothes and jewels, music, art, and dancing. Most of all, however, they both loved the message of the gospel. In fact, Katherine had written a book in which she explained how long it had taken her to understand that message because she had been trying to merit heaven by doing good things. When people do that, she said, they treat everything Jesus did as unimportant.

Usually, in the mornings and evenings, everyone in the palace— family, visitors, and servants—gathered to read the Bible and pray. Both Katherine and Jane attended faithfully. On the other hand, some said that Thomas often skipped these family devotions. Jane enjoyed life with the Seymours and learned much while she was under their care.

Jane and Katherine shared a passion for books, fine clothes, art, music, and especially for the gospel.

About nine months after Jane moved in with the Seymours, something wonderful happened to Katherine! She had always wanted to have a child and found out that God was going to answer her prayer. A baby girl was born in August 1548, and Katherine named her Mary. It was a happy time for all, but not for long. Sadly, only six days later, Katherine died.

PHOTO BY ERIC HARDY, USED BY KIND PERMISSION OF SUDELEY CASTLE

Katherine's tomb

For many days, Thomas Seymour was heartbroken and couldn't think of anything else, so when Harry Grey asked him to send Jane home, he did. A few days later, however, Thomas changed his mind. He still had great plans for the young girl. In fact, he was hoping to arrange a marriage between her and King Edward.

At first, Jane's parents were not sure that it was a good idea for her to return to Thomas's house. Now that Katherine was dead, the only woman who could take care of her there was Thomas's mother, who was very old. They were also concerned because they felt that Jane needed more discipline than she had been getting with the Seymours. Finally, they agreed to let her go. Jane was happy and wrote a letter to thank Thomas for his offer. She said he had always been to her "a loving and kind father."

Sudeley Castle,
where Jane lived for some time
with Katherine and Thomas

## CHAPTER TWO
# Times of Trouble

Jane had been back in Thomas's house for only two months when trouble started. Edward Seymour thought that his brother Thomas was trying to kidnap the young king. He also didn't like it that Thomas was trying to arrange a marriage between Jane and the king without the council's approval. He accused Thomas of being a traitor, and at that time in England traitors were killed.

In the end, Thomas was found guilty and executed on March 19, 1549. He didn't consider himself a traitor. In fact, he thought he was the only one trying to do what was best for King Edward.

John Aylmer

Jane didn't leave any writings to tell us how she felt at this time, but we can imagine it was difficult for her. Back at home, she kept her mind on her studies. Her main teacher, John Aylmer, was a kind and gentle man who appreciated women's talents at a time when some people thought women were not fit to study or write. She learned all the basic school subjects, including Latin and Greek, two ancient languages that were necessary at that time because many important books had not been translated into English. She also learned some Hebrew, so she could read the Old Testament of the Bible as it was originally written, as well as other languages, such as French, Italian, Chaldaic, and Aramaic.

Her Italian teacher, Michelangelo Florio, had been forced to leave Italy because of his belief in the gospel. He told Jane many stories about his difficult life in Italy, where he had almost been killed for his faith. Hearing these stories, Jane was moved to tears and prayed for all the Christians who were still risking their lives in that difficult country.

Jane loved studying. In fact, visitors were often surprised to see how much she could learn at her young age. One of these visitors, Roger Ascham, was once amazed to find her sitting alone in her room, while everyone else was out hunting, reading a difficult book written in Greek. Bradgate Park was a land filled with deer, and hunting was a popular family pastime.

Roger Ascham

Jane had met Ascham before, when she was staying with the Seymours, so she was happy to see him again. When he asked her why she was all by herself, she explained that she was disappointed that her parents preferred sports like hunting to the joys of reading and studying. She also complained about their strict discipline. To her, it seemed that they wanted her to do everything just as perfectly "as God made the world." We don't know if they were really stricter than other parents or if she was just resisting their correction.

Jane explained to Roger Ascham why she preferred studying to hunting.

We know, however, that her teacher had some concerns about her teenage years, an age when people, he said, "are inclined to follow their own ways." He was particularly concerned about the way women, even as young as Jane, often appeared in public "dressed and painted like peacocks." In fact, he was so concerned that he wrote to a famous Reformer in Switzerland, Henry Bullinger, to ask him to encourage Jane not to follow their example. Since Harry Grey was one of King Edward's counselors, Jane probably had many occasions to visit the royal court during special events when fashion was very important. On the other hand, from her letters to Bullinger and other Reformers, we know that she respected and tried to follow their advice.

Henry Bullinger

SIDONIUS, WIKIMEDIA COMMONS

Archbishop Thomas Cranmer

While Jane continued to study at home, King Edward and his council worked hard to make sure the message of the gospel spread throughout the kingdom. To teach people to worship God in a way that was closer to the teachings of the Bible, Archbishop Thomas Cranmer (the most important man in the Church of England after the king) published the Book of Common Prayer as a guide that all churches were supposed to follow. It was a well-written book full of inspiring prayers, helping people to keep their eyes focused on Jesus and His sacrifice. You can ask your parents to read some of these prayers to you.

Some of these changes, however, were difficult for the people, who were used to the sense of mystery of the ceremonies and Latin prayers and to the candles, pictures, colors, and smells of wax and incense that filled the churches in the past. The Reformers instead wanted to draw people's attention away from images and things they could see, smell, and feel, and direct them to God's Word, using a language that everyone could understand. Most people, however, like what is familiar to them and have a difficult time accepting new ways.

One person in particular was very angry about these changes—Princess Mary, Edward's older half sister. The Church of England had started when King Henry divorced Mary's mother, so Mary hated this new religion and wanted the country to return to the Roman Catholic Church. In fact, she flatly refused to obey her half brother. King Edward threatened Mary but couldn't do much because she had the protection of her powerful cousin, Charles V, emperor of the Holy Roman Empire, who hated the Reformers.

Queen Mary I

It was difficult for a young king to rule over a country so deeply divided. Poverty was also a big problem in England, and when people are poor, they often rebel. In 1549, a group of noblemen, led by Lord John Dudley, who later became Duke of Northumberland (we will call him Northumberland from now on), accused Edward Seymour of being a major cause of these problems. For that reason, Northumberland took his place as head of the royal council, acting in the place of King Edward, who was still too young to rule by himself. Seymour tried to resist and was finally executed.

Most problems seemed to quiet down for a while until, in February 1553, King Edward became ill. At first it looked like a simple cold. Edward was strong and active like his father, a lover of sports and hunting, so no one worried much. Soon it became obvious that the illness was much more serious. Perhaps it was an infection that developed from a cold but couldn't be cured because there were few medicines at that time. When it seemed possible that Edward might die, he and his men became worried about England's future.

According to the will left by King Henry VIII, if Edward died without children, Princess Mary would become queen. Edward didn't think Mary had a right to be queen, because his father had divorced her mother. There was, however, a much deeper worry: he knew that Mary would lead the country back to the Roman Catholic Church. With this in mind, he worked hard to write a new will and appoint a new successor. He had to write and rewrite a few times, because he wanted the document to be just right. He knew that he could change his father's will if he could just get this new document approved by Parliament, a group of counselors who had the power to make laws.

King Edward worked hard to write a new will.

## CHAPTER THREE
# A Heavy Crown

Who could take Edward's place instead of Mary? It had to be a close relative. Lady Jane had already been on the list of possible heirs, and Edward knew that she really loved the gospel.

In the meantime, a marriage had been arranged between Lady Jane and Guildford Dudley, one of Northumberland's sons, and it was celebrated on May 25, 1553, followed by great festivities. Guildford was a handsome young man with good manners, a little older than Jane. We don't know how Jane felt about the marriage. As most noble girls in her day, she had to accept her parents' decision. Soon after her wedding, however, she became ill and had to spend some time in bed. She believed it was due to some poisonous greens that were put in a salad on purpose to harm her, but we don't know who would have done that.

On June 21, while Jane was still sick, King Edward finalized his will. Realizing that he had much less time than he had thought, he nominated her to be the next rightful queen without waiting for the approval of Parliament. To those who objected, he replied that he was the king and had the power to do so.

He finally died on July 6. As with the death of his father, the news was kept secret for a few days. In the meantime, realizing that Mary could cause serious problems, Northumberland sent one of his sons with three hundred men to capture her and bring her back to London. To his surprise, his son discovered that Mary had suspected their move and had left for a safer place.

On July 9, Jane, still recovering, received a strange visit from her sister-in-law, who told her to go to a place in West London called Syon House, the home of the Dudleys, where she would "receive that which had been ordered by the king."

The two girls traveled to Syon House by boat on the river Thames. There, they had to wait until the next day for Northumberland and other councilmen to arrive. Lady Jane had heard about King Edward's will from Guildford's mother, but in front of all those men she felt very confused. Jane's and Guildford's mothers had to come and explain to her what was happening. When all those councilmen knelt at her feet, promising their loyalty, she dropped to the ground, sobbing over her cousin's death. At first she protested, because she didn't really want to be a queen. But then she asked God to help her rule to His glory and service and for the good of the kingdom—if that was His will.

Jane and her sister-in-law traveled on the river Thames to receive a message from the king.

The next day, heralds made proclamations at four important places in the city, announcing the king's death and Jane's succession to the throne. As most kings and queens of England before her, Jane traveled in a large procession of long boats on the river Thames all the way to the royal apartments in the Tower of London. There, she entered with great ceremony, with Guildford at her side and her mother behind her, holding the train of her dress. To the watching crowd, this was strange because normally a daughter would hold her mother's train. It was also odd that the crowd was not cheering. Most of them didn't understand why Jane, and not Mary, was now queen.

TREVOR HART

The Tower of London

Jane walked to the Tower of London with great ceremony.

Jane was especially troubled when, inside the Tower, the high treasurer brought out her crown to see if it fit well. At this point, she refused to wear it. She had never tried to become queen, and the idea was still strange to her.

She was also troubled when the treasurer talked about having a crown made for Guildford. Maybe Jane thought that her marriage had been a plot to make Guildford king. Or maybe she wanted to make sure her position as queen was first confirmed by Parliament, as Edward had desired. After that, Guildford would have become king automatically. After some thought, she said that she didn't want to make him king, but just duke. This surprised Guildford and made his mother very angry.

Jane refused to make Guildford king.

The next day the royal council met to discuss important matters. It was then that a messenger arrived, sent by Mary, with a letter demanding that the council recognize her as queen. Immediately the men replied that Jane was the rightful queen, and Mary had to accept it. They also wrote letters to local officers, explaining how they should not listen to Mary, who didn't have a right to the throne. Jane signed all these letters.

Mary's support, however, was growing, and it was obvious that John Dudley's son needed help to capture her. The council discussed who should lead the troops. Should Jane's father be the leader? Jane said no. She wanted him near her. Instead, she approved the decision to send Northumberland, even if he was clearly unhappy about it.

Jane sat at the head of the council as they chose the right man to send to fight Mary.

DAN NELSON

Framlingham Castle,
where Mary found refuge and gathered her troops

As Northumberland moved closer to Mary's place of refuge, he heard some discouraging news. Mary had at her disposal about ten thousand well-trained soldiers sent by local gentlemen who supported her cause. Then, even worse, the English navy took her side, providing her with more soldiers and heavy guns. After considering all options, Northumberland realized he just had to retreat.

When the news of Mary's victory reached London on July 19, the crowds reacted with great joy. Instead of keeping silent, as on the day when Jane was proclaimed queen, they celebrated by throwing hats in the air, leaping, dancing, and tossing money around. Jane's council switched sides, and Jane was practically left alone.

Mary had about ten thousand trained soldiers ready for battle.

## CHAPTER FOUR
# Prisoner

If Mary was the rightful queen, as she claimed to be, then Jane was now considered a traitor because it appeared that she had tried to take her place. Soon after the announcement of Mary's victory, Jane and Guildford were taken as prisoners and held in separate places in the Tower. Jane was sent to the nearby house of the Tower's jailer, Nathaniel Partridge, where she was mostly confined to her room. As Mary's cousin, she was treated nicely and had some servants to take care of her. Northumberland was also arrested on his way back to London and held prisoner.

On August 3, Mary rode triumphantly into London in a chariot, accompanied by about eight hundred noblemen, her half sister Elizabeth, and one hundred of her men. Again, a great crowd gathered to cheer her. Within the next two weeks, she chose the members of her council and sent more of Jane's supporters to prison, condemning some—including Northumberland—to die as traitors. She decided, however, to pardon Jane's parents and Northumberland's sons, except Guildford.

For Jane, in some ways leaving the crown was probably a relief. At the same time, she was concerned not only about her life, but also about the future of the churches in England. Once, when some visitors came unexpectedly to Partridge's house while she was at dinner, she invited them to sit and talked to them for some time, eager to

FROM *LADIES OF THE REFORMATION*, BY REV. JAMES ANDERSON, 1855

Lady Jane at dinner in Partridge's house

hear any news and especially if the churches in London were now worshiping according to the teachings of the pope. "Some are," the visitors replied.

To Jane, the greatest surprise was to hear that before he died, Northumberland had returned to the Roman Catholic religion, hoping to please Mary and save his life. In her eyes, he was the main person responsible for what had happened, so how could he hope for mercy? Many people were returning to Roman Catholicism at that time—some out of fear of punishment and some because they liked to follow the religion of their rulers. Jane told her visitors that she prayed that God would help her never to forsake her faith "for love of life," even if doing so would give her, a young girl, many more years to live.

Even though Mary's counselors and friends encouraged her to put Jane and Guildford to death as traitors, she didn't want to do that. Jane had explained to her how she had never wanted to become queen, and Mary believed it was true. In spite of that, she agreed that Jane and Guildford should be tried in court.

On November 13, Jane and Guildford were tried together with other people who had been accused of being traitors. It was a very humbling experience because they had to walk slowly for about one mile from the Tower to the Guildhall under the stares of the people. A man walked in front of them holding an axe. On the way to the Guildhall, the axe's blade was pointing away from the prisoners because they had not yet been declared guilty. At the trial, however, they were all condemned to die, so on the way back the blade was pointing toward them. During both the walk and the court trial, Jane remained quiet. Even when they announced that she was going to die, she didn't show any emotion.

MYRIAM BARDINO

The Guildhall in London

Jane, Guildford, and other prisoners had to walk slowly to the Guildhall to be tried as traitors.

She had, in fact, determined to live her last days and die as a true Christian, not only keeping her faith but also showing confidence in God. She didn't know how long she would have to wait before her death or—if the queen wanted to show mercy—her release. As she waited, she wrote a long prayer to God, showing her faith that, in spite of all her sins, His "Son Christ shed His precious blood on the cross" for her. Because of this, she knew that all her troubles were meant only for good. "I am absolutely persuaded that all that Thou doest can only be well," she said. She also quoted many Bible verses, showing that she knew the Scriptures well.

By the time Christmas came, Mary was firmly established as queen. All the changes made by her half brother, Edward, had been reversed. Roman Catholic ceremonies were restored, and many efforts were made to replace the statues and images that Edward had wanted removed. Most of her enemies had been killed and imprisoned. She then became a little more lenient toward Jane, allowing her to walk in the garden every day for exercise.

Jane prayed, remembering that Christ had died for her on the cross.

It is believed that Jane's father used this table and chair while he was hiding inside an oak tree.

Around that time, Mary made a decision that shocked the English people. She decided to marry a foreigner—Philip of Spain, son of Emperor Charles V. This was terrible news for a people who were very proud of their independence. Soon, a small group of noblemen united to form an army against her, to kill her or at least force her to leave the throne. Three of these people were Jane's father and uncles. Their plans didn't work, and they had to flee for their lives. Jane's father hid inside a large, hollow oak tree and his brother under a pile of hay, but they were eventually discovered and taken to the Tower as prisoners.

After trying to dethrone Mary, Jane's father hid inside a large, hollow oak tree.

CHAPTER FIVE
# Ready to Die

At this point, Mary thought it was too dangerous to keep Jane and Guildford alive. As long as she was in the Tower, other people might try to put her back on the throne. By the time Jane's father arrived at the Tower, he discovered that Jane was sentenced to die two days later, on February 12.

Mary believed that for people to go to heaven, they had to respect the authority of the Roman Catholic Church and obey its teachings. She was very concerned because Jane did not believe this. Before Jane's execution, Mary sent a monk named John Feckenham to convince her to change her mind. Jane, however, could never do that. She talked for a long time with Feckenham, explaining that the teachings of the church should never contradict the Bible. "I ground my faith on God's Word and not upon the church," she told him. Feckenham returned a few times, but Jane hung on to her convictions.

FROM STORIES FROM ENGLISH HISTORY BY M. JONES, PUBLISHED BY T. NELSON AND SONS, 1868

An artist's view of the meeting between Jane and Feckenham

Finally, Jane prepared herself to die. During her last few hours, she wrote letters to her sister Katherine and to her father. She might have written other letters, but we have only these. She wrote to her sister that she rejoiced because she knew that she would soon "lose a mortal life" to "win an immortal life." Jane also sent Katherine her copy of the Bible, which she considered "more worth than precious jewels."

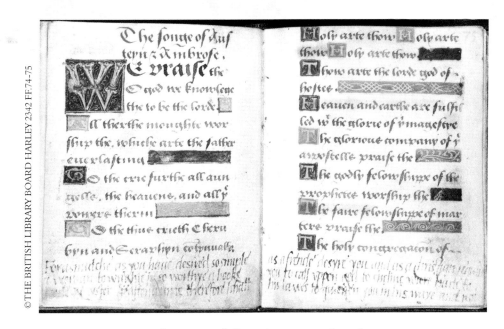

A page of Jane's prayer book

To her father, she wrote a loving and encouraging letter in her prayer book, then asked an officer of the Tower to pass it on to him after her death. The officer agreed to show her letter to her father, but since Harry Grey had also been condemned to die, he asked if he could keep the book and if she could write a message for him too. Jane then wrote a very caring message, encouraging the officer to follow God's truth.

On the day of the execution, it was decided that Guildford should die first. He asked to see Jane, but she refused because it would have been too painful. Maybe she was also afraid that she might lose the calm spirit she was trying to keep until the end. Besides, she knew that they would soon meet in heaven.

Then it was Jane's turn. She walked to Tower Green, the place chosen for her execution, with her prayer book in her hands, reading all the way. On the scaffold, she turned to the people, explaining that she had been condemned to die by law but had never wanted to be queen. She also confessed she had sinned before God, neglecting His Word and loving herself and the world too much, and thanked Him for giving her time to repent.

"I pray you all, good Christian people, to bear me witness that I die a true Christian woman," she said, "and that I look to be saved by none other means but only by the mercy of God and the merits of the blood of His only Son Jesus Christ." Finally, she asked for prayer but added, "while I am alive." Jane was pointing out that there is no use in praying for the dead, a practice in the Roman Catholic Church.

Jane told the people she was dying as a Christian,
saved only by God's mercy, in the merits of the blood of Christ.

She then read Psalm 51 out loud and thanked Feckenham for keeping her company. Affectionately, and teasing a little, she told him that during her last few days she was more bored by him than frightened by death. Then she knelt by the block and tied a band around her head, blindfolding her eyes and keeping her hair off her neck at the same time. In the darkness, she felt lost. "What shall I do? Where is it?" she said, until someone came to guide her. Her last words were the same that Jesus cried from the cross: "Lord, into Thy hands I commend my spirit."

Jane's reign was so short and contested that she is never remembered as Queen Jane, but always as Lady Jane Grey. Still, her story has been the subject of many books, poems, paintings, and movies, encouraging many Christians with the thought that the same God who preserved and strengthened Jane's faith until the end will do the same for all His children.

Elizabeth I reigned after Mary

At a time when people had to follow the religion of their ruler, both Jane and Edward felt responsible to make sure that their religion was true according to the Scriptures. At the end, their plans seemed defeated. During Queen Mary's reign, many Protestants were executed, most people were forbidden to read the Bible, and everyone had to worship according to the traditions of the Roman Catholic Church. Mary ruled, however, only five years.

During the reign of the next queen, Elizabeth I, the Book of Common Prayer written by Archbishop Cranmer was used again, and the Church of England became similar to what Lady Jane and King Edward had desired. Until today, in England, as in all the world, God has been preserving His teachings and His church, whether big or small.

# Time Line of Lady Jane Grey's Life

*1537* – Lady Jane is born.

*1547* – King Henry VIII dies, and his son, Edward VI, succeeds him on the throne.
Lady Jane moves in with Thomas Seymour and Katherine Parr.

*1548* – Katherine Parr dies.

*1549* – Thomas Seymour is executed for treason. Lady Jane moves back home.

*1553* – In January, King Edward becomes sick.

- In April, plans are made for the wedding of Lady Jane and Guildford Dudley.
King Edward writes his will naming his successor, who is different
from the successor his father's will names.

- On May 25 Jane marries Guildford.

- On June 21 King Edward signs his final will, saying that Jane will take his place
as queen of England.

- On July 6 King Edward dies.

- On July 9 Jane is taken to Syon House in London, where she learns about Edward's
death and will.

- On July 10 Jane, as queen, moves to the Tower of London after a long procession
on the river and by the pier.

- On July 19 news reaches London that Mary has won the support of the
people to be queen. Jane and Guildford are imprisoned.

- On August 3 Mary enters London as queen.

- On November 13 Jane and Guildford are officially condemned to die as traitors.

*1554* – On February 10 Jane's father and uncles are taken prisoners and jailed in the
Tower for plotting against the queen.

- On February 12 Jane and Guildford are executed.

# Did you know?

- Jane is often called the "Nine-Day Queen" because she ruled for a very short time. Since normally a king or queen begins reigning at the death of the former king or queen, we can also say that Jane ruled for thirteen days from the time King Edward died.

- At the time of Lady Jane's birth, around 2.3 million people lived in England. Today, there are almost 52 million people. In those days people lived in small communities, scattered throughout the country. London was the largest city, with about 50,000 people. Today there are more than 7.5 million people in London.

- It was common for noble families in Lady Jane's day to send their children to live with other noble families. This was done for different reasons. Sometimes the children could get a better education. Sometimes they could get better training in certain skills, such as military skills for the boys and ladylike occupations for the girls. Often, parents thought that living with other families would also teach the children more lessons in submission.

  Children from poor families left home early too, but for different reasons. Often the parents had so many children that they could not feed them all, so they sent the oldest children into the world to find work. It was very dangerous, and they rarely had a chance to go back home. Children of poor families usually had to work in the home by the time they were six. If they stayed at home, they often ended up supporting the family as the parents became old.

- Younger children played many of the same games we still enjoy today. In winter, they liked to throw snowballs and play with sleds and ice skates. In the summer, they chased butterflies or filled reeds with water and blew through them to spurt it out on each other. Hide-and-seek and ball games were very common. Sometimes players pushed balls with wooden sticks, a little like we do today in field hockey. Boys liked to ride on sticks as play-horses, fight with wooden swords, or pretend they were in tournaments. Other popular toys were tops with strings and dolls. There were also tiny plates and pitchers girls used to play house, and small horses with riders for boys to play war.

❧ Some of the good manners Jane was taught, like other children at that time, included speaking to an adult only in answer to a question, standing straight, thanking others for compliments, and kneeling by her parents at night to receive their blessing.

❧ During Lady Jane's life, many explorers traveled to faraway lands and brought back interesting objects, new foods, and exotic animals like parrots and monkeys. Kings, queens, and very rich people liked to have a collection of these animals in their properties. Since the thirteenth century, the Tower of London had a mini-zoo with bears, elephants, leopards, kangaroos, ostriches, and lions. King Henry VIII kept canaries and nightingales in cages. We have portraits of young Edward VI and Catherine of Aragon, Mary's mother, each carrying a monkey. Around 1524, turkeys were brought to England from South America, and they soon became a very popular dish.

❧ Rich and noble families, like the Greys and the Seymours, usually lived in large palaces full of activities and people. Jane probably dined often in the home's great chamber, waited upon by carvers, cupbearers, and servers. On many occasions, there were probably entertainers and minstrels to bring joy to the meals. In each of these homes there was also a chapel with a chaplain who led the religious services and family devotions.

❧ King Henry VIII is famous because he had six wives, one after the other. He divorced two and executed two more. Of the other two, one died after having a baby and the last one,

Katherine Parr, survived. Some remember them by the rhyme, "Divorced, beheaded, died; divorced, beheaded, survived."

❧ King Henry VIII had a difficult personality and made some unjust decisions. Still, Thomas Cranmer and Katherine Parr loved him and tried to help him. Katherine took care of him when he was very old and suffered from a painful wound that never healed. As the king was dying, he called Thomas Cranmer to his side. When Cranmer arrived, Henry was already unable to speak. He might have expected the Roman Catholic ceremony typically used in those occasions, but Cranmer reminded him that his trust should be in Christ alone. When Cranmer asked him to give him a sign of his trust in Christ, the king squeezed his hand as hard as he could. Some say that Cranmer stopped cutting his beard as a sign of mourning over the king's death. If you look at different portraits of Cranmer, you will see that his beard kept getting longer.

❧ Thomas Cranmer stayed in prison two years after his trial. The leaders of the Roman Catholic Church put so much pressure on him that he finally denied his true beliefs and signed some papers that said he agreed with them. God's Spirit, however, convicted him of the sin of doing that. On the day when he was scheduled to give a speech to all the people and explain how the Protestant religion is wrong, he did just the opposite. This infuriated Queen Mary, who condemned him to be burned at the stake. Cranmer went cheerfully to his death, putting his right hand into the fire as a sign he had repented of signing papers against his true faith. "This hand has offended," he said out loud so everyone could hear.

❧ Katherine Parr almost lost her life for the gospel. While she was living with King Henry, some officers noticed that her religious convictions were getting closer to those of the Reformers. Because some of these convictions went against the teachings of the Church of England, they issued a warrant for her arrest. By God's providence, the messenger carrying the warrant dropped it on the ground, and someone loyal to the queen told her about it. Katherine then went to talk to Henry and told him she had been studying these new teachings so she could discuss them with him, learn from him, and take his mind off his troubles. After her explanation, Henry forgave her.

❧ Religion was a major part of life in Lady Jane's times. Everyone went to church. Those who could read often had a prayer book, sometimes called a book of hours, which usually included prayers, some quotes from the Gospels, some psalms, and many colorful illustrations. Jane took her prayer book with her to her execution.

❧ The Book of Common Prayer is still a very important document for the church. Many famous prayers that you hear from time to time are taken from this book. For example, in a wedding, the words "from this day forward, for better and for worse, for richer and for poorer, in sickness and in health,

to love and to cherish, till death us do part, according to God's holy ordinance," come from the Book of Common Prayer. When someone is buried in the ground at a funeral, the minister may say the words "earth to earth, ashes to ashes, dust to dust," and they are from the same book.

❧ During Lady Jane's lifetime, doing laundry was a huge chore, and it was put off as long as possible. Clothes were washed with ash and hot water. Linens were often boiled. Men, women, and children had a few pairs of detachable sleeves that they could change when the others got dirty, instead of changing their whole outfit. Some also had one pair of simple sleeves to use in the house and a fancier pair to wear outside. Richer ladies like Jane could afford several detachable sleeves to change as they liked to give a whole new look to any dress. A custom since the Middle Ages, women gave one of their sleeves to the knight they favored so he could wear it as a banner on his armor.

# Jane's Letter to Her Sister

I have sent you, my dear sister Katherine, a book. On the outside, it is not trimmed with gold, but inside it is worth more than precious jewels. It is the book, dear beloved sister, of the law of the Lord. It is His testament and last will, which He left to us poor sinners, and it will lead you to the path of eternal joy. If you read it with a good mind and follow it with an earnest desire, it will bring you to an immortal and everlasting life. It will teach you how to live and how to die. It will give you more than you would have gained by the possession of your poor father's lands. If God had prospered him, you would have inherited his lands. In the same way, if you study diligently this book, using it as a guide for your life, you will inherit great riches that the covetous will never take from you, the thief will never steal, and the moth will never destroy.

Desire, sister, to understand the law of the Lord your God. Live to die, that by death you may enter into eternal life, and then enjoy the life that Christ has gained for you by His death. Don't think that just because you are now young your life will be long, because young and old die as God wills.

Strive, then, always to learn how to die. Defy the world, deny the devil, despise the flesh, and delight yourself only in the Lord. Repent of your sins, and yet don't despair. Be strong in faith, with humility. With St. Paul, desire to die and to be with Christ, with whom, even in death, there is life.

Rejoice in Christ, as I trust you do. Since you call yourself a Christian, follow as closely as you can in the steps of your master, Christ Jesus, and take up your cross. Lay your sins on His back, and always hold Him near.

As for my death, rejoice as I do, my dear sister, and consider that I shall be delivered of this corruption and put on incorruption, for I am sure that I will, for losing a mortal life, gain a life that is immortal life. I pray that God will grant you this life in His time and will give you His grace to live in the fear of Him and to die in the Christian faith. In God's name, I exhort you never to swerve, through hope of life or fear of death, from this faith. If you deny His truth to lengthen your life, God will deny you and shorten your days. If you hold faithful to Him, He will prolong your days to your comfort and His glory, to which He is bringing me now and will bring you later, when He is pleased to call you. Farewell again, my beloved sister. Put your trust only in God, who only must help you. Amen.

Your loving sister,
Jane Dudley

# Acknowledgments

Jane's story has been told and retold many times over the centuries, becoming increasingly embellished and entangled in myths. The greatest challenge in writing this book about her life has been clearing away these myths to discover what seems certain. It is a daunting task that I could never have achieved without the kind and patient help of scholars such as Dr. Eric Ives, emeritus professor of English history at the University of Birmingham and author (among other titles) of *Lady Jane Grey—A Tudor Mystery*, and Dr. J. Stephan Edwards, historian, who have read the manuscript and made invaluable comments.

I am also grateful to Dr. Diarmaid MacCulloch, professor of history of the church at the University of Oxford and author (among other titles) of *The Boy King: Edward VI and the Protestant Reformation* and *Thomas Cranmer: A Life*, for taking the time to explain to me some perplexing issues about the complex and shifting times of the Reformation. Given my undependable memory and stubborn nature, these men have exhibited a rare graciousness.

Another challenge in writing this book has been obtaining photos, which are often associated with exorbitant fees and heavy restrictions. Thankfully, I have found many people willing to help (their names appear next to each picture), and I can't even begin to express my gratefulness for their generosity. I also want to thank Dianna Ippolito of Besame Photography and Dustin Wilson for taking photos of the scenes following Matt Abraxas's sketches; the James, Taylor, and Andersen families for posing; and my friend Heather Chisholm-Chait for reviewing the manuscript.

A final thank-you goes to the 3rd-4th graders at Christ United Reformed Church for listening to a reading of this book and giving their opinions and suggestions, to my husband Tom and my children for their encouragement and patience, to all my church family for their prayers, and to Dr. Joel Beeke, Jay Collier, Steve Renkema, Annette Gysen, and all the Reformation Heritage Books staff for their continued vision and support.